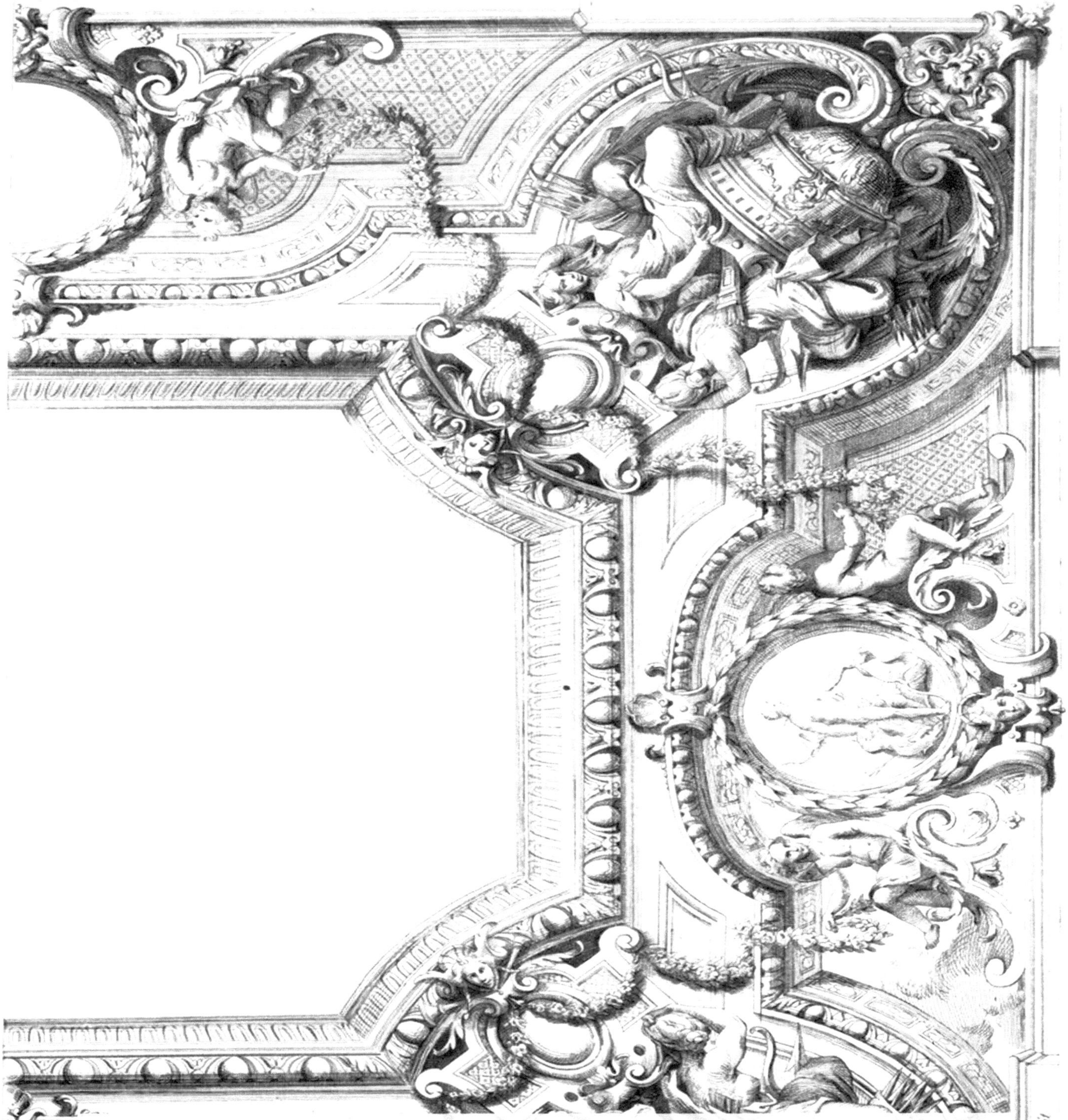

This book is possible due to the Public Domain access granted by the New York Public Library. The designs are undated but antique drawings from Paris. They come from the book “Nouveau livre d'ornments, pour l'uitillitee des sculpteurs, et orfeures..” (The New Book of Ornaments for Use by Sculptors and Goldsmiths...)

This book was created by Don Landes-McCullough.

First Printing: 2016

Parasol Publishing
1300 SE Park Crest Avenue
Vancouver, WA 98683

heyUkid
CHILDREN'S BOOKS

PARASOL PUBLISHING

Available through Amazon.com, CreateSpace.com and other retail outlets.

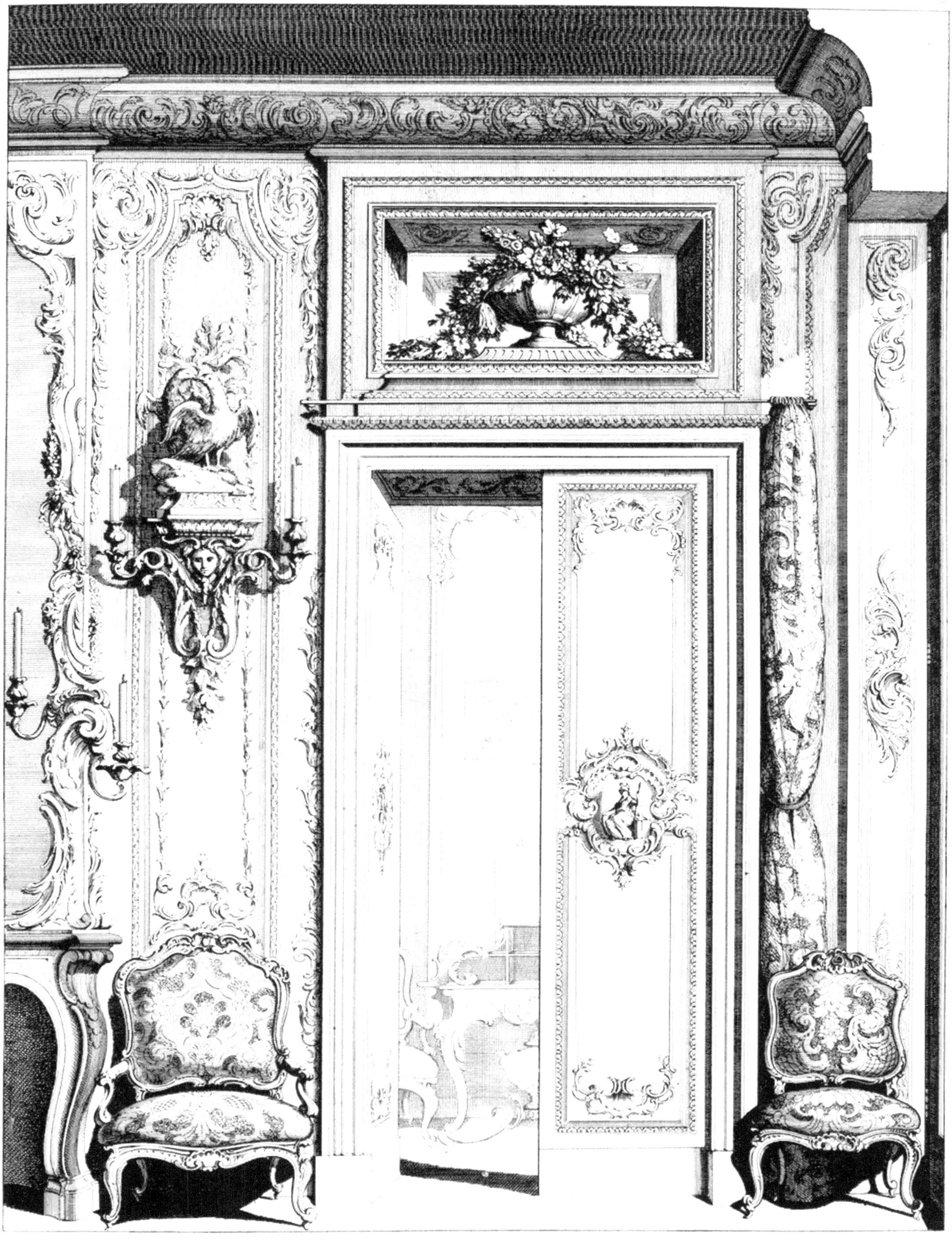

4

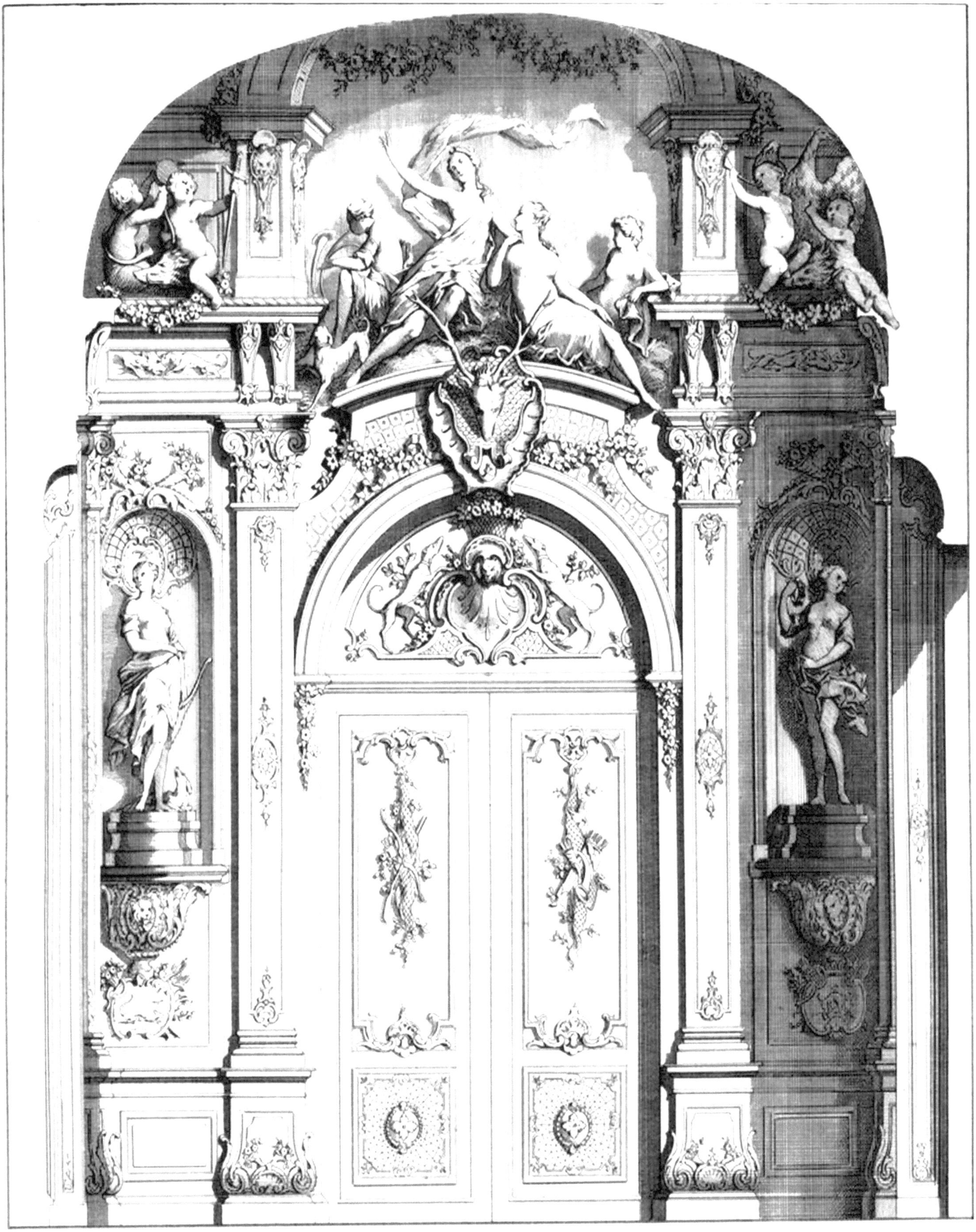

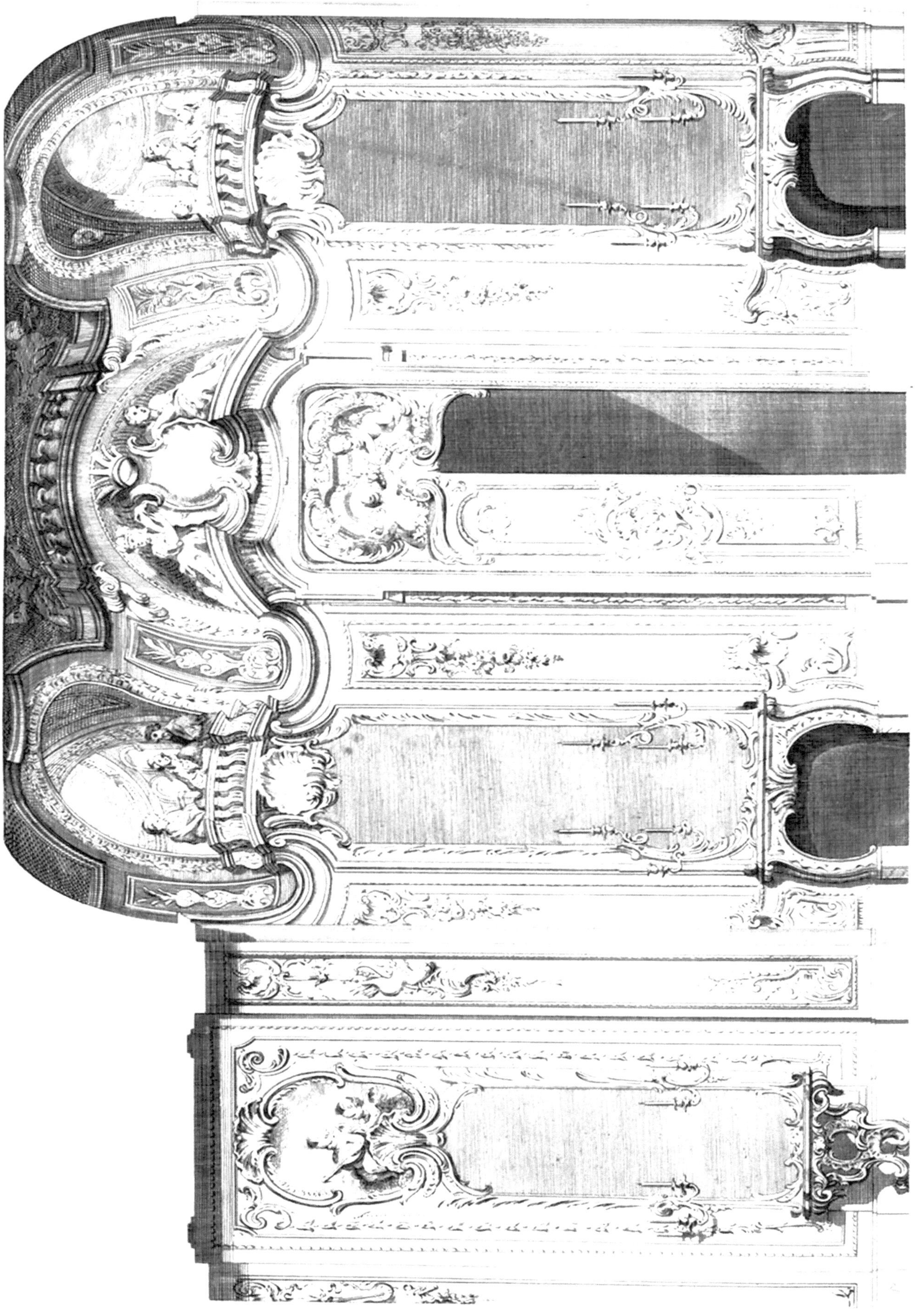

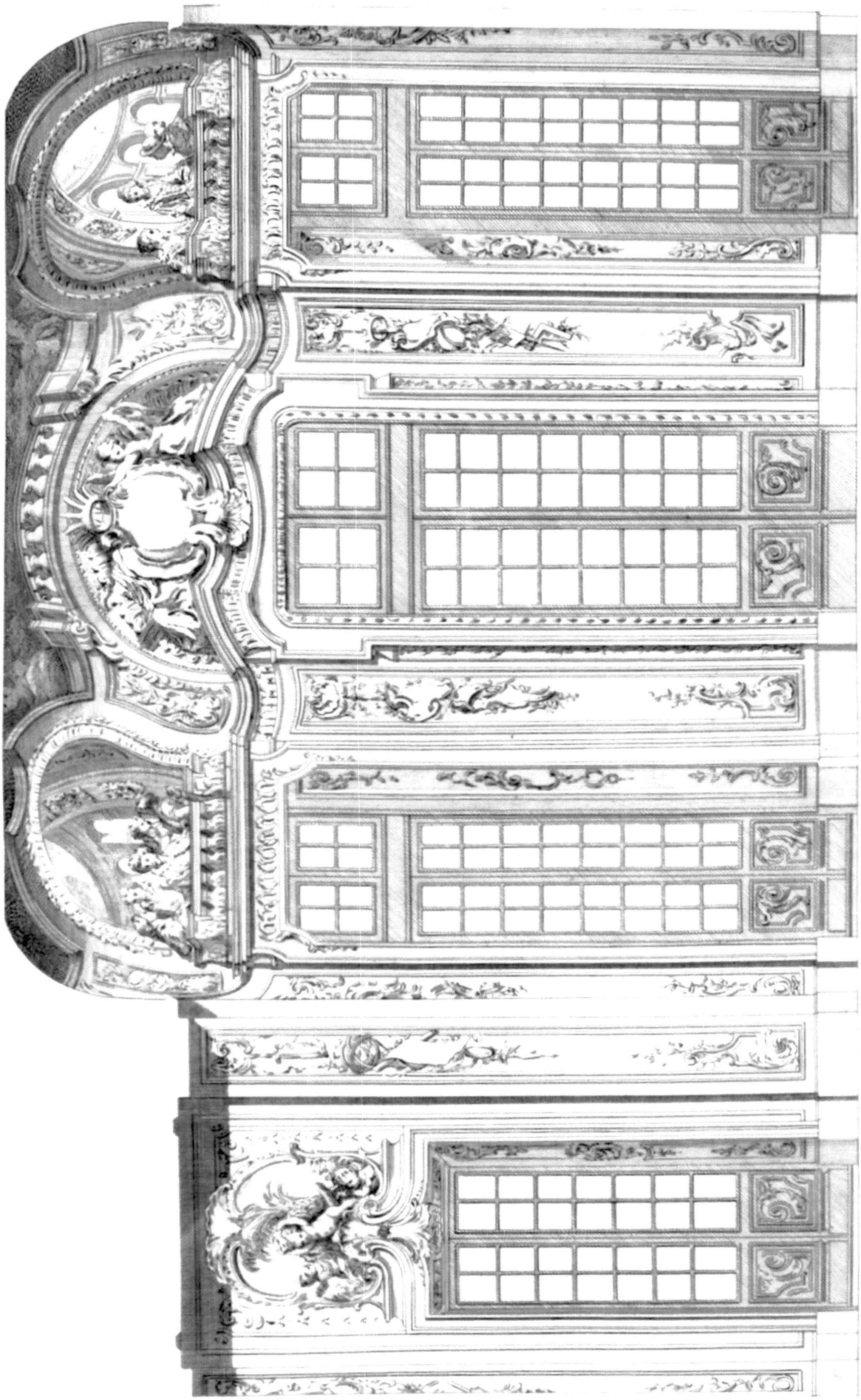

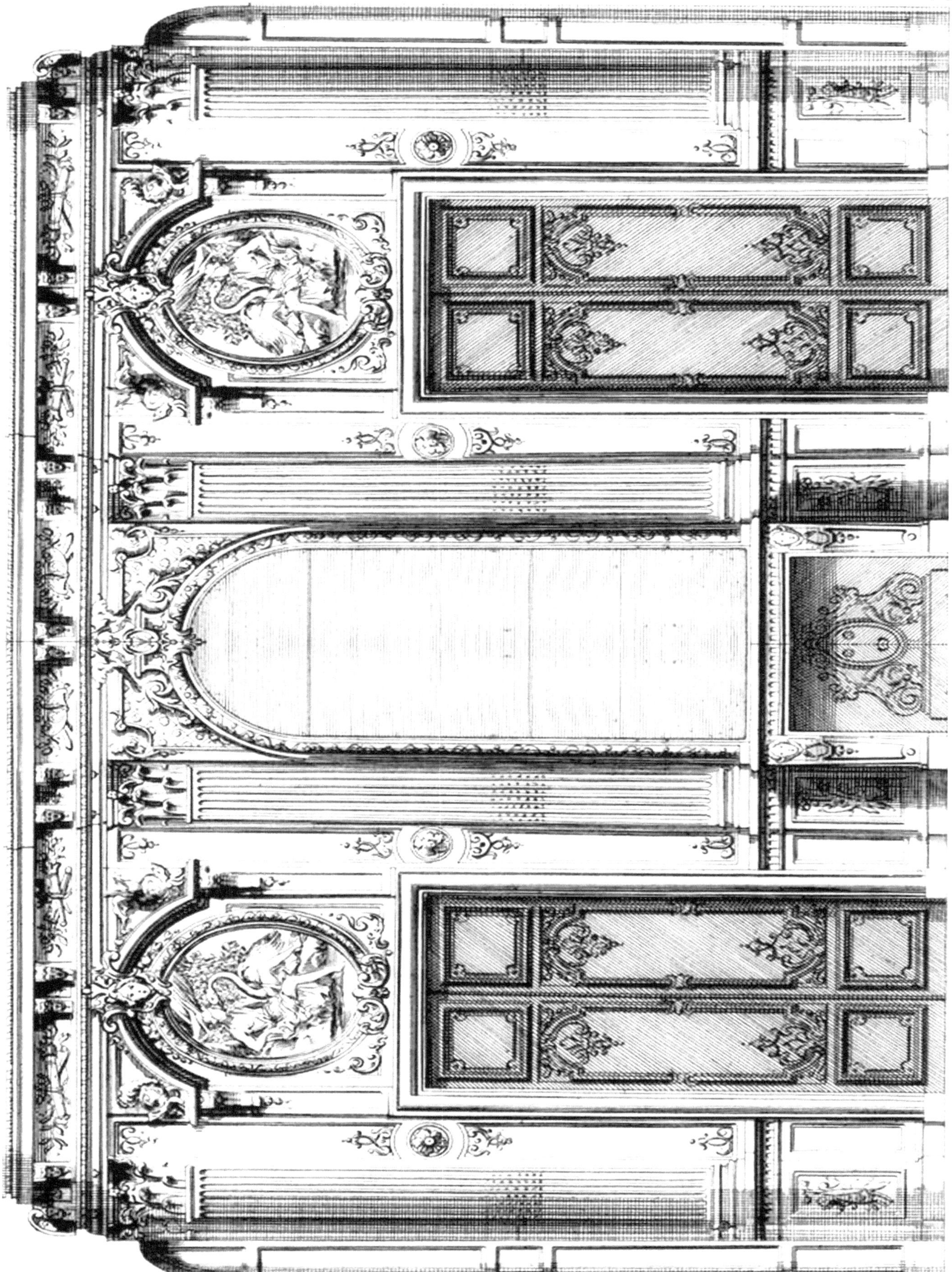

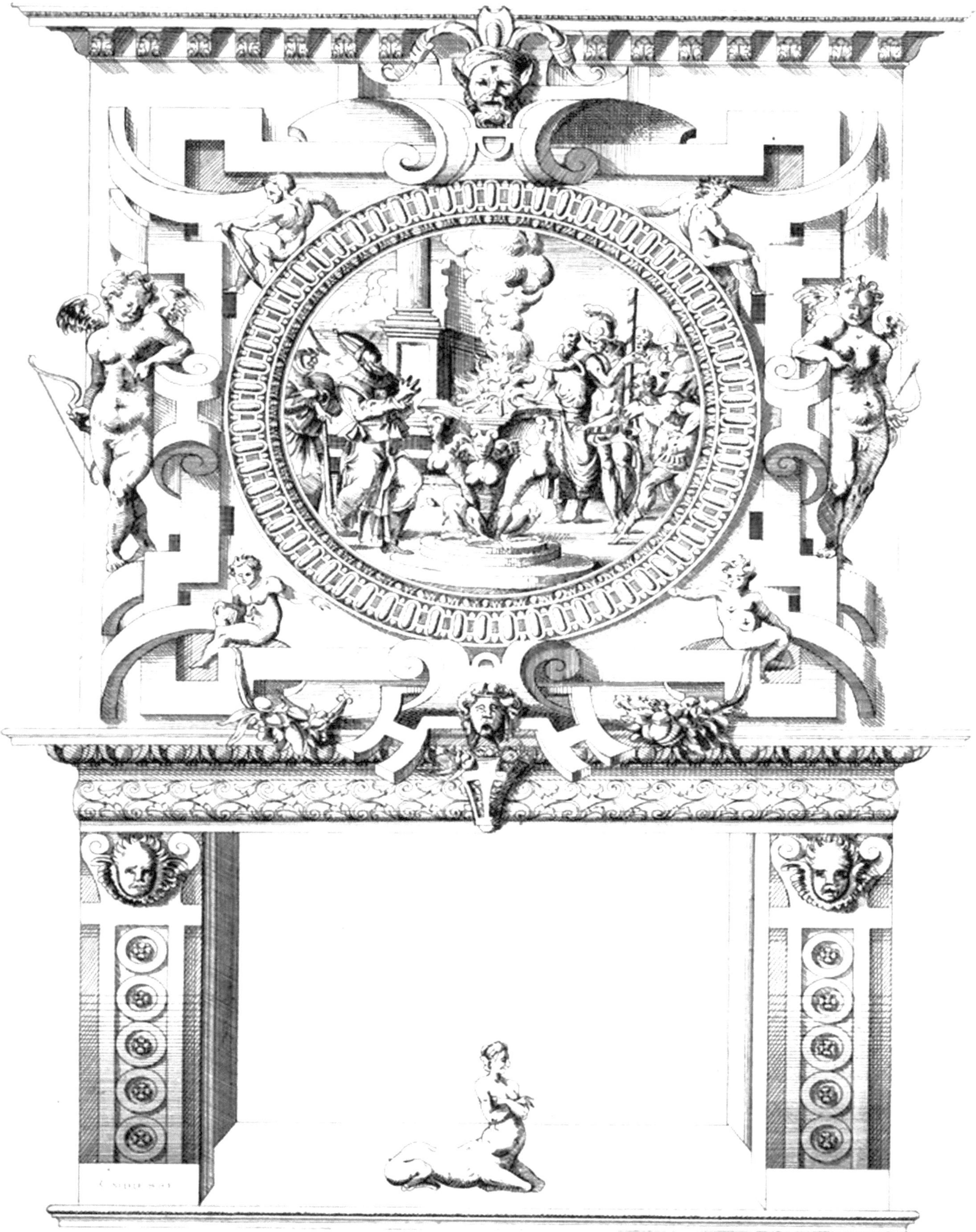

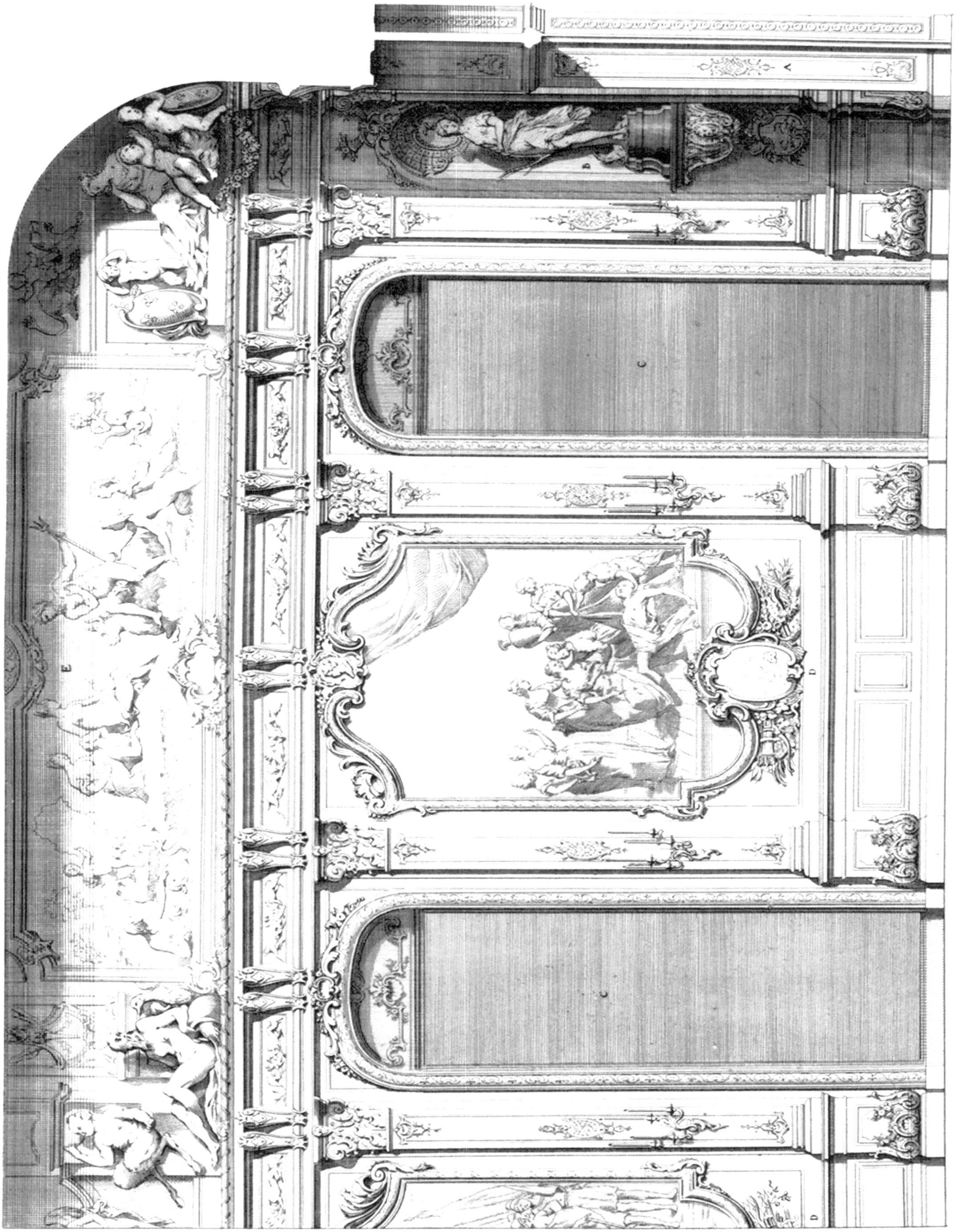

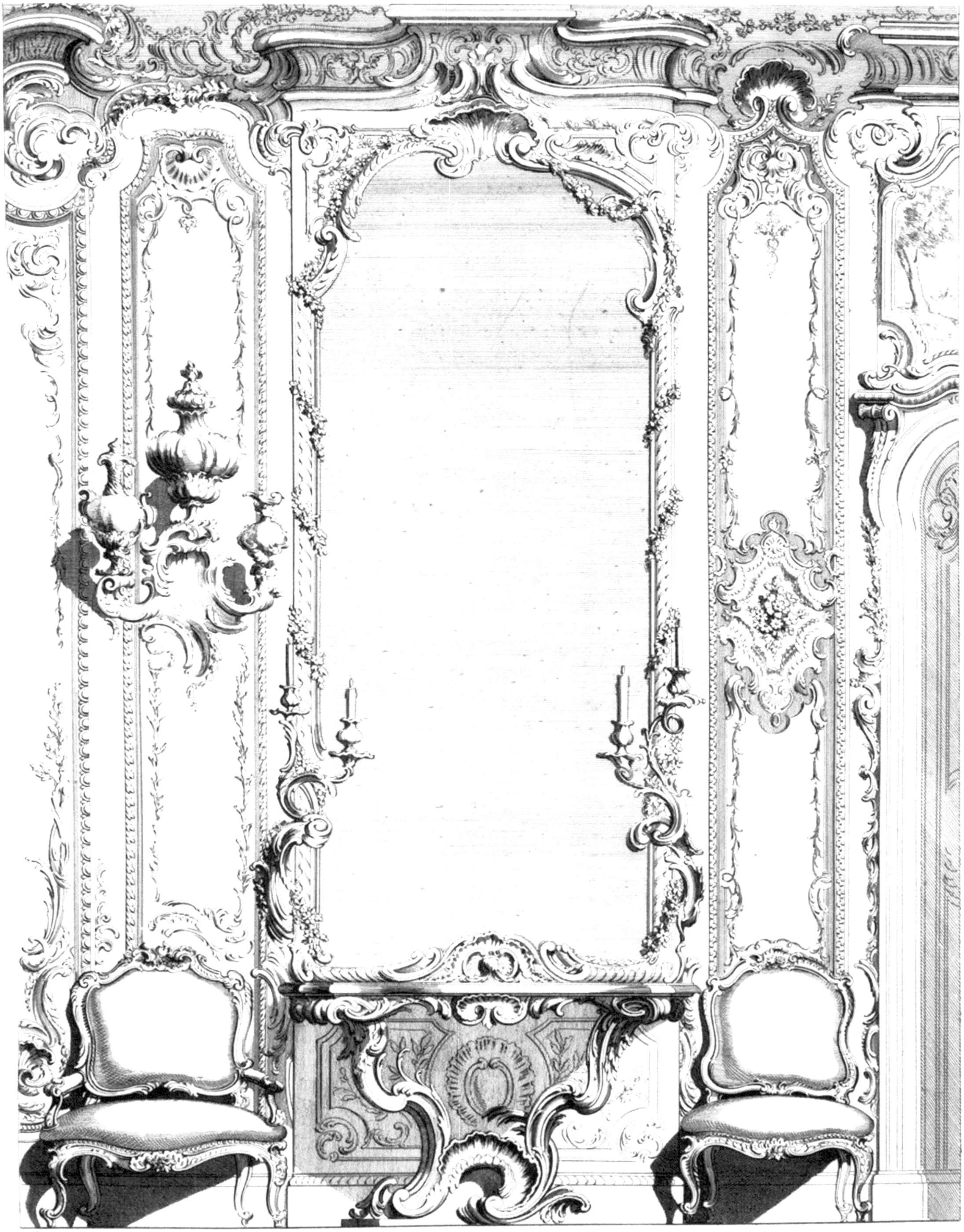

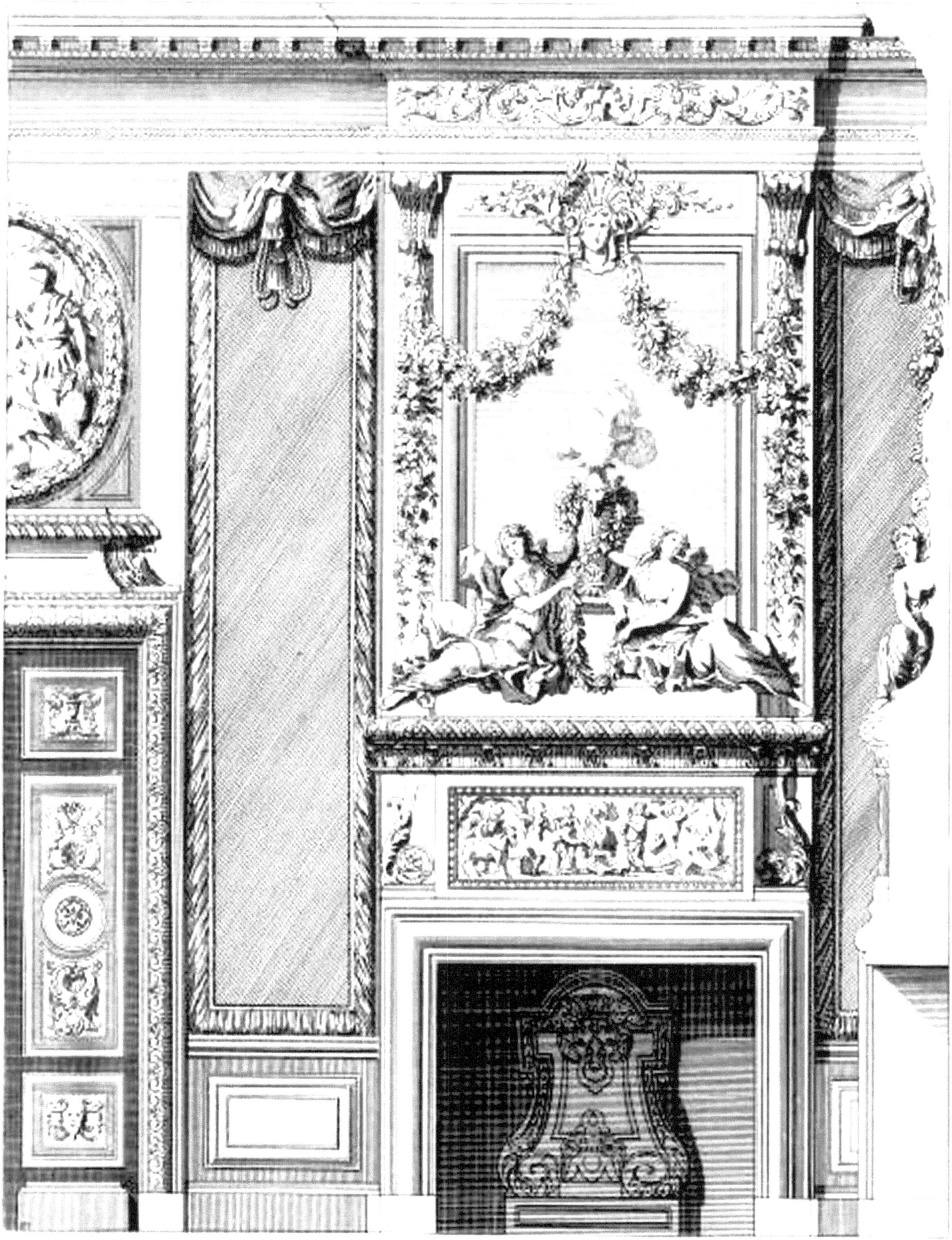

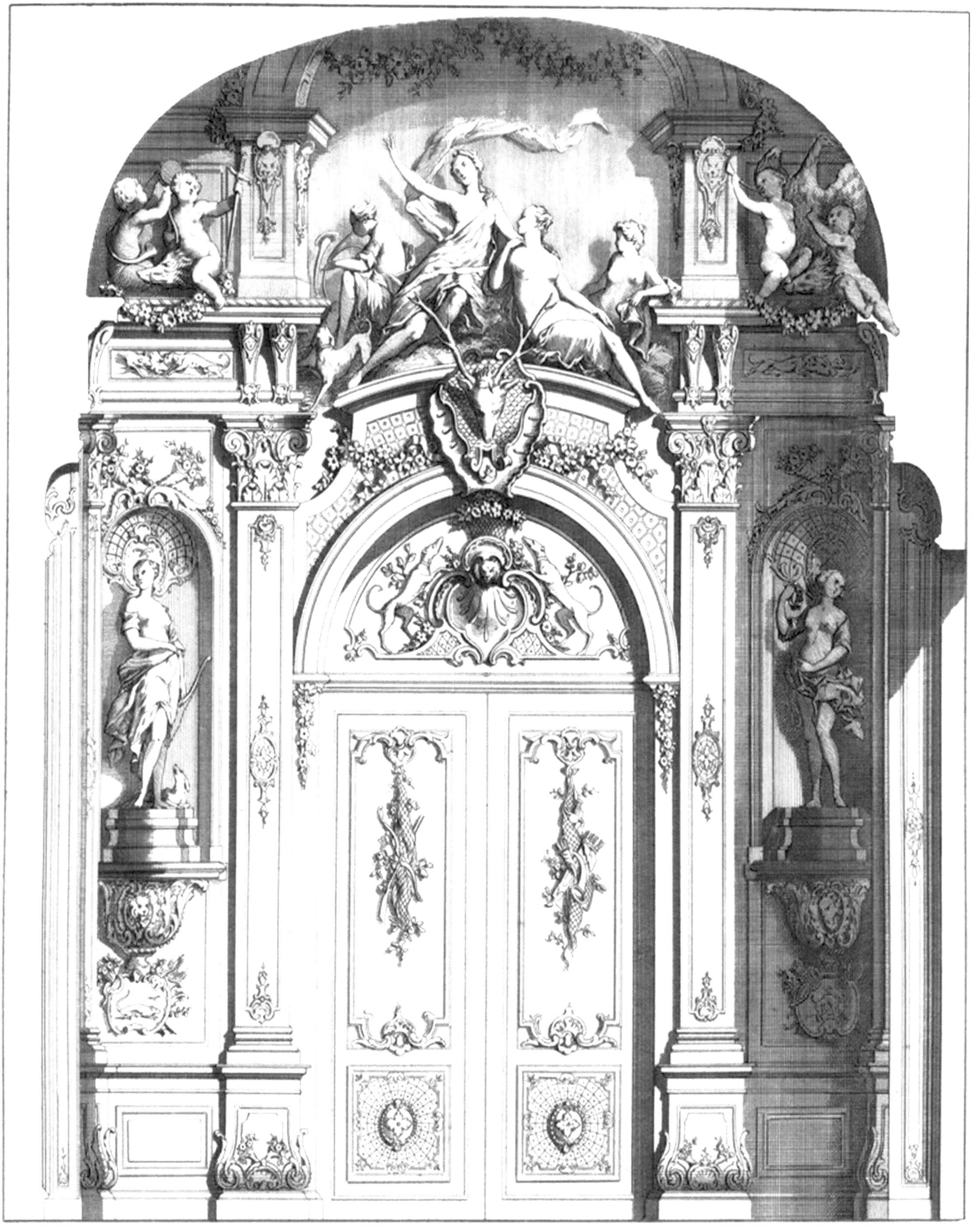

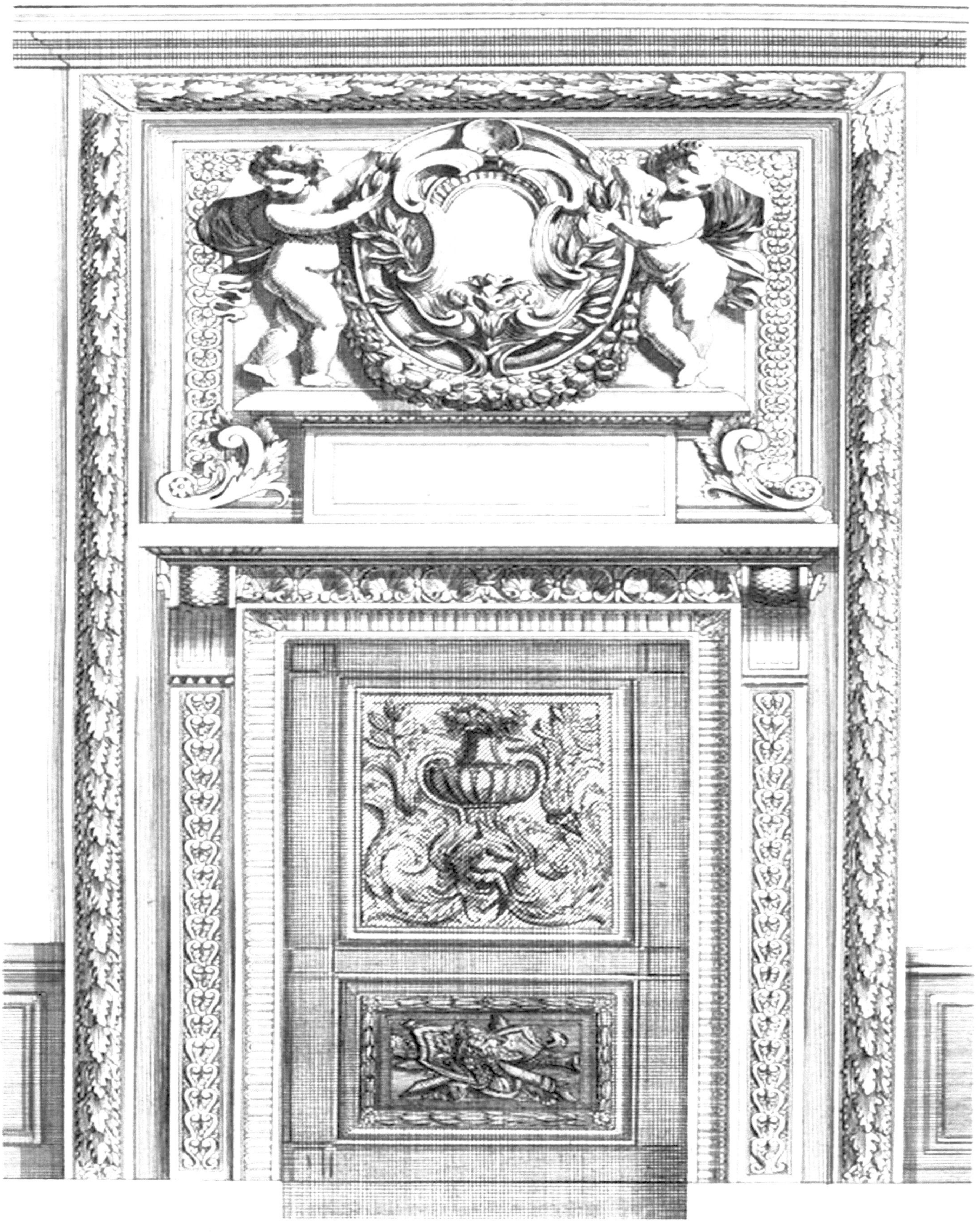

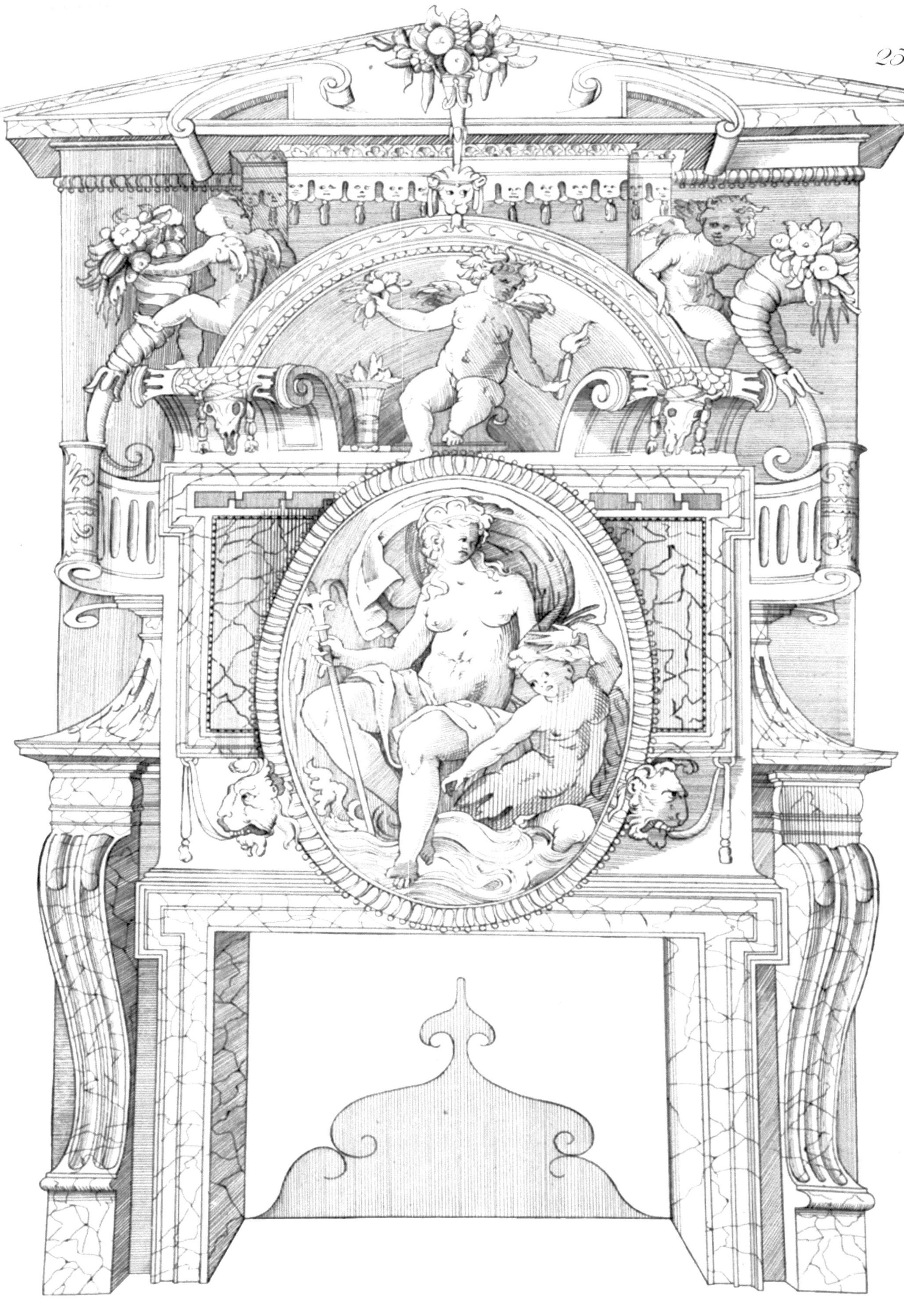

www.ingramcontent.com/pod-product-compliance
Lightning Source LLC
Chambersburg PA
CBHW050412180526
45159CB00005B/2246
* 9 7 8 1 5 2 3 8 6 5 4 1 3 *